WHEN I MET MY SOUL

SILPA SRIKUMAR

Made with ♥ on the Notion Press Platform
www.notionpress.com

"All the humans who find it difficult to communicate their emotions are remembered in this song."

Dedicated To: Late Ms.Susheela

Ms.Susan

and to all my constants.

Contents

Preface   *vii*

Acknowledgements   *ix*

1. Embed   1

2. Be In The Land Of Living...   2

3. Dwindle   3

4. Memoir   4

5. Secret Self   5

6. Dreams, A Dream?   6

7. Open Window   7

8. Leaves...   9

9. Angst   10

10. Woods   11

Preface

This collection of poems explores my experiences as well as how they affected me. As it has been a ten years adventure , I hope it will touch your heart.

Acknowledgements

This is for people who had the guts to do what they truly felt was right...

1. EMBED

These four walls are shrinking;
I can no longer see my own shadow,
The colors I've seen in your eyes are fading.
Allow me to float in your eyes with your colors.
Every morning, I shed my leaves because I had lost my home.
Be my tree, a place where I can be cherished for who I am.
Be my strong root, on which I can stand when the howling gales blow.
These four walls are shrinking,
where I can no longer water myself.
Where I am unable to fertilize my land,
the seed within me seeks to grow.
The land in me is parched and longing for rain.

2. Be in the land of living...

I have been dead for a while
I want to breath again
Let the sun shine bright on me
Let the rain pour freshness to my soul
I want my body to feel my soul and let it fire.
Let the moon sing lullabies for me
And I want to look at the moon and smile again.
Let the breeze touch me and take away all my sorrows.
As I want to live again...
As I want to breathe again...
As I want to feel my soul again…

3. DWINDLE

As I told you about my secrets, my thoughts vanished.
The dreams that had lain dormant for a while had vanished, along with
the tears you had shed in the face of the gloom.
Your self-doubt about my own existence and thinking has since subsided.
It disappeared!
It has vanished from view!
When I stood like a firmly planted tree among all the storms, it
vanished!!!

4. MEMOIR

You are my lovely recollection.
Give me the opportunity to hold your hand once more, once more, and
again as I wonder how life evolves.
For better or worse, the world around me altered.
I miss riding in the scooter with you and hearing your stories while we go
for ice cream.
I miss the concern you had for me.
We frequently played together over lunch, as I recall.
I tickle you, and your fish fry is stolen.
I still recall the mango dishes you made and how we split it evenly.
I recall the scary movies we saw together.
how you led me to my bedroom.
I wish I could have another chance to relive my childhood with you!

5. SECRET SELF

Let me look at your face
And forget the world for once.
Let me hold your hands so tight
So that you will never leave me .
Let me fly as high as I could
But I want to come back to the nest to hold you tight.
Let me listen to your voice as it soothes my heart.
Let me look into your eyes and stay for a while
As I could not express myself through words.
Let me listen to your every thought!!!
And let my heart smile!!

6. Dreams, a dream?

Let the rain fall down
To give life to your dreams.
Let the water flow freely
To the land, for green.
Do not let the thunder be
An obstacle on your way.
Let the lightning strike your mind.
And let them give , the power
To face the future.
Let the rain fall down
To awake your dreams.
Let leaves catch
every raindrops.
Let your dreams flow like a river.
Drive your life along with your dreams, like a ship on a sea.
Let your dreams touch the sky
And shine like the sun.
Let your rays awake others
To make a new world of love and peace.
And let them bloom like flowers...

7. OPEN WINDOW

Waited for you so long.
Looking at nature, crying
became a habit for me
I cried for you looking at sun
Through an open window.
When the night falls
And when all fall asleep
I woke up, middle of night
With your memories you gifted
I cried for you, looking at moon
Through an open window.
When the sun rises
I was still in my bed
Hugging my teddy bear
Because I missed you badly
Looking at sun rays through
As open window.
But I realized that
You have gone to the
World of unknown
Where there will be
No societies that bother
Caste....Money.....Status......!
But you came like breeze

That touched my face and hair
And still waiting for your
Call at night.....beside window....

8. Leaves...

The leaves have fallen!
But the roots are still strong.
"What made you sturdy?" mumbled the fallen leaves to the root.
The sunshine: rains: breeze!
Sunshine?
Why did you not burn out?
The fire within me is stronger than of.
And what about the rain?
The soil is more compacted.
The breeze ?
Roots were stronger,
Even when the ground shook fiercely...

9. ANGST

Heart rate is rapid.
Am I timid?
Why is it that I fear people?
Why is my heart beating quickly and I'm sweating?
Is it anxiety?
Fear of being judged?
Why is it difficult for me to converse with strangers?
Am I nearing my word limit?
Why am I unable to laugh or win?
Where's my roof?
Hello?
Which moment am I?
Anxiety kissed my cheeks !

10. Woods

I perceived the sky
While I was wandering
Through the forest.
Blue covered it.
A rabbit I met,
Stole my carrots, though!
I spotted lovely birds
And dreamed of flying with them,
But I ended up stuck in a desert!
I became lost on the way
To my destination
And ran into a tiger
In the thick woods.
She lead me.
But she vanished out of thin air.

www.ingramcontent.com/pod-product-compliance
Lightning Source LLC
Chambersburg PA
CBHW021200130726
47988CB00004B/1691